Top The

Charts

How to Successfully Self-Publish Your

Urban Fiction E-Book

Pen N Paper

This book is for all the self-published urban fiction authors looking to become an Amazon Bestseller author

Contents

Why I Wrote This Book 1

Chapter 1 Audience...3

Chapter 2 Writing..7

Chapter 3 Standalones Or Series 18

Chapter 4 Website Maybe? 22

Chapter 5 Promoting Your Book.....................24

Chapter 7 Reviews 29

Chapter 8 More Promo 32

Chapter 9 KDP 34

Chapter 10 How to Get Paid...........................38

Chapter 11 Resources and References 41

Promoters 42

Graphic Designers 44

FB Groups for Urban Fiction Authors 46

Editors, Proofreaders and Test Readers 49

Chapter 12 The Fruits of Your Labor.................51

Note from the Author...53

So you are an urban fiction author. Congratulations on your journey. You have come to the correct place. I know you have a love for writing and putting your words in print or on the screen drives you, but you want to make money as a published author. What good is the greatest story ever written if nobody sees it or you don't reap the financial benefits for your hard work? Look no further this is your literary lifeline.

Following these steps, you will easily become one of the top players in the urban fiction literary industry.

Do you want to become a household name? Do you want to make enough money to pay your bills and live the life as an author that you deserve? Are you tired of receiving royalties under $20? Are you tired of being under a publisher who can do no more for your career than you can for yourself? If you said yes to any one of these, this book is for you!

If you are hungry for success with writing a great book and being compensated well let's not waste any more time. It's enough room at the table for all urban fiction authors to eat. Let's get to the business of getting your best seller published now!

The first step when to self-publishing is to know your audience. Although many writers say they write for themselves, best-selling authors also write with their audience in mind. The beauty of this arrangement is that if you do write what you would enjoy reading, you then can find like-minded people who will also love what you have written.

As a self-published author, you can write about anything you want because you are the boss. That sounds good, doesn't it? Yes, you are the boss. As a boss, you have a responsibility for the public to know who your company is, in your case, it's you the author and the publishing company. Your readers are your audience.

One of the best places to find readers is online. Your social media is a great start to find readers. You can start by posting stories on posts. If you get lucky your story could possibly go viral. If not, you still will have feedback and exposure from readers wanting to know more. Creating a post is absolutely free!

Readers who like your post also tend to share your posts. Relish the moment. Make sure to interact with your supporters.

Positive interaction is the key.

Never ever come off as messy. I mean messy sells books, but you don't want to tarnish the brand that you are working towards building for your audience.

It is also important to note that everyone is not going to like what you write so make sure to market to the correct audience and stay focused on your goals.

***

How do you target your social media audience?

For the sake of Facebook or Instagram, my two personal favorite social media sites to interact and share my books, this is how you use social media:

Identify your target audience.

Survey your customers. Create polls and ask questions.

Determine your target audience size.

Find Your readers and connect.

Find Your target audience in Facebook groups. (We will come back to this)

Create posts for your target audience.

Create a FB page, IG, Twitter or IG page just for your readers. It does not hurt to have one of each. A website or a blog is also very useful but for now we are focusing on the free social media stuff. You should be building an audience while working on your book. Have an audience first. It is not a good look for you as an author to be begging for readers!

Don't drop your books in peoples' inbox or DMS! That is a quick way to get blocked, therefore cutting off your chance to network. I can't stress positive interaction enough! This is your brand so make sure that you are representing the best you at all times when interacting with your audience.

Now that you have an audience it is time to get to the good part! It is now time to write your book. Let your pen be filled with nothing but dope ass stories! Write the best book you can, then proofread it thoroughly -- and consider hiring a professional editor. Matter of fact don't consider it, do it. Make editing your book a top priority.

It is very possible to become an Amazon best-seller with a self-published book. It is highly suggested and recommended that self-published authors should use editors especially since there is a notion that most authors of this genre don't use editors. Hiring an editor can be expensive but it does not have to be. Prices range from as low as fifty dollars, yes, I've seen it done, to several hundred, to a few thousand dollars per book, the investment will more than pay for itself if your book becomes a bestseller. You will get what you pay for! Don't forget this is your brand so there are no excuses. Of all the steps to skimp on this one is not the one. Trust me!

Try looking for editors that may take payment plans or work with you. If you can't afford an editor check around for test readers and proofreaders. Use Grammarly. Do peer reviews. I would say save up until you can afford a good editor, but some will skip this step. I'm confident that you won't.

Editing is very critical to your work. If all else fails I will provide a list in the back of the book that you can check out. These editors are not being sponsored or anything, but I know that they are in high demand so please check them out.

When writing your story, the most important thing is not to procrastinate. Try to write every day. Set a minimum of at least five thousand words a day. That way you will have at least twenty thousand words in a week, well in five days. If you write seven days a week you will exceed your word count goals. You can most certainly write more but this will be enough to write your book in two weeks. Following this process, you should be able to craft a book that is at least forty to sixty thousand words, the average length of the bestselling urban fiction books on Amazon.

It won't hurt you to write longer books but that's a good starting point. Another important thing to note is that longer books pay more. That does not mean to fill a book with a bunch of crap that will take away from the essence of the story, but a longer book will bring more coins with Amazon.

Currently, authors in the urban fiction genre are writing novellas and short stories right at the thirty thousand mark and that's fine too. The only word of advice I have for novellas is that you need to be consistent with writing them if you want to see a financial return. With shorter books be prepared to deliver more books.

Consistency is another driving factor in delivering a bestselling book. You will need to write and put out good books. The books have to be something the readers love and enjoy. So get to writing.

First, break the project into small pieces. Next, settle on your big idea. Create a unique and fresh storyline that will have the readers full attention. Sure there are tons of books similar to yours but make your book stand out. After you have birthed that great idea, construct your outline. Some authors don't use outlines but it helps keep the story in order. Just because it started out that way does not mean the story has to end that way. If an outline is not your thing consider making notes in a notebook. You can email yourself, or use note apps on your phone. I swear by One Note, I can use that to make notes on the phone and my sticky notes on the computer are saved on my phone. Such a lifesaver. You don't have to use any of these methods, but they have been proven to get results for me when crafting a book.

When I published my first book I was writing everything by hand in notebooks and then typing it up, but it is 2019. Time is money. Work smarter not harder. I'm not sure what your budget is as a self-published author but you will more than likely start doing the bulk of the labor yourself unless you outsource tasks.

After making your story notes and ideas now it's time to execute the goals. Put some fire under that pen and deliver that hot story. Make sure to write daily. Set a firm writing schedule. Even if you don't want to, do it anyway! If you don't know what to write listen to music or watch TV to get a little motivation. Stick to the schedule. When the characters start talking you don't want to miss a thing. As a self-published author you may have to fit the time into your daily life but trust me after a while it gets to be easy. Remember to keep your eye on the prize. You want to create a good book and you want to be paid well for doing so.

Once you have written for dear life if you write at least five thousand words a day in seven to ten days you will have a book. It's possible to write two books in a month but now we are focusing on at least one a month. Not considering rewriting and editing, establish a deadline. After your book is done you will have to edit and make those changes. This could take a few weeks or a month. The key to this is to stay ahead of the game.

For instance, if you start your book on the first of the month and take two weeks to complete it, no later than the twelfth of the month the book should be going to the editor. If the editor has your book for a week, two at the maximum when the book comes back make those changes immediately. Of course, this is just an example, I know real life happens but for the sake of this book and timelines follow with me.

The book may need to be written over in its entirety once it comes back from the editor, after all, there are three steps to writing. They are prewriting, writing and post writing. You will not be perfect, hell practice makes perfect. While your book is out to the editor it's is important to be working on the next book. This is very important if the book is part of a series.

When writing series, which are popular in urban fiction you could even consider writing all three or four parts at once so it can be released back to back. But let's not get ahead of ourselves.

Your great story will also need a title. Catchy titles help sell books. Nothing draws a reader in more than an intriguing title. An interesting title can be a powerful motivator for people to 1-click your book. Also, keep in mind, the title has a strong effect on whether or not your book shows up for a search term, so keep this in mind.

A great cover will also help sell your books. Although the title and cover are important that can come after the book is written. This is a step that can be worked on while the book is being edited or while going through the writing process.

Another thing to focus on writing is the synopsis and book description. Now would be the time to focus on writing taglines. Most authors dread writing them so why not write it early so you can have a chance to edit that and make changes as well.

After the title and the cover, the most important marketing material for your book is the description. The book description is what readers see when they pull your book up on Amazon. It's crucial that this short paragraph be right. This needs to be well crafted and edited because it's a major factor in whether the reader buys your book or not.

The book description is the pitch to the reader about why they should buy your book. It is sales copy to get them to see that the book is for them, or not, and then make the purchase.

The first sentence should be something that will grab your desired reader and make them take notice. Start off with some action, grab their attention!

Next state the problem or question your book addresses, you show that you solve or answer it, but you also leave a small key piece out. This piques the interest of the reader and leaves them wanting more. Never give them too much, just enough to leave them wanting to read your book. After crafting your description start working on keywords and hashtags to use that relate to your book. They will also be another selling point for your book.

After organizing your description and keywords, write with confidence. Be creative and write with a purpose. Everything will work out. You

are a future best selling author!

Now we are getting to the meat and potatoes. Write more than one book. Books bring you bucks! If you are writing as a career move you will need a catalog. One book will get you a bestseller but not necessarily paid. We will discuss metrics more in this chapter.

Anyone who reads one of your books -- and loves it -- is more likely to purchase your other books than someone who has never read your work before. From my own experience, part of my success was writing a series of novels and not just relying on one novel to become a best-seller.

This is where we are going to discuss what you are writing. Are you going for a novella, a novel, which would be considered a standalone or are you going to write a series? Let's address what you will be writing.

First, there is a short story

3,500 - 7,500 Words

The most important difference between a short story, novella, and a novel is the word count. They are often popular in short story challenges on FB, IG and even Twitter. Short stories are an excellent marketing technique to introduce a story and draw in readers. People can read those in a sitting.

The novella

17,000 - 40,000 Words

It can involve multiple sub-plots, twists, and characters. It too can be read in a sitting. Novellas are the current "in thing" or trend in Urban Fiction. Keep it short and sweet. Keep in mind if you are going to be publishing these the readers will want more and more so be prepared to publish more often. Novellas are a good way to build your catalog

The Novel

40,000+ Words

The novel is one of the more common works. It is also known in Urban Fiction as a standalone. As an English major, you will never see me say that my book is a standalone! Nope, it's a novel! That is the proper literary term. A novel often involves multiple major characters, sub-plots, conflicts, points of view, and twists. A novel is usually no shorter than 40,000 words, yet a novel can spread over 80,000 – 120,000 words.

Finally, there is a series

A book series is a sequence of books having certain characteristics in common that are formally identified together as a group. Series are money makers for authors in this genre. Readers love them! People have written up to ten book series!

Decide what you are going to write and write as if your life depends on it. Whatever you choose to write make sure to be consistent. At the end of the day write whatever you choose, just make sure that it's your best writing!

Chapter 4 Website Maybe?

Launch a website where people can find out more about you and fans can contact you. Place links to your books on the site, with descriptions and links to the Amazon store. I'm not sure what your budget is so a website may not be the thing for you just starting out. That is a personal choice. Once you are an established author you definitely want to create a website or pay someone to set you up with one.

If you can't afford a paid site you could always look into free alternatives. Blogging may also be a good start. Try out a free site like Wordpress. I am simply not going to spend too much time on this chapter because we still have the issue of publishing the book at hand. A website is useful to promote and direct readers to so they can stay up to date on your new works and order paperbacks and other swag but for now, let's stick to the basics.

Adding to the website, create an email list and place it prominently on your website so fans can sign up. Encourage readers to contact you and let you know what they liked most -- and what they liked least -- about your book. Keep this feedback in mind while writing your next book. Even without a website, a mailing list is useful to keep your fans updated on your works.

Congrats again! You are on your way to living the lifestyle you deserve as a published author.

There is no such thing as too much promotion! You are a brand and books are your business. Always engage your readers on social media websites like Facebook and Twitter. Give readers a chance to get to know a little about you. Although not necessary, it is good to have a personal page and a fan page on FB.

With the fan page you are able to boost post for larger audiences to see. If this is something that you are new to it can be outsourced to marketers. If that is not in your budget play around with it to see how it works.

Even without paying for boosted posts, FB is your friend. Tag your friends and followers, with permission though. You don't want to be reported as spam or end up in FB jail. Ask your followers to share your post. Another great way to promote your brand and your books on FB is to hire FB promoters. I will list some well-known promoters later. They are not sponsored by me but they are some of the best when it comes to this. The promoters will make sure to get your book seen and in front of the right readers. This is a sure way to reach the goal of a best selling book.

What you don't want to do is just drop links all day. Interact and network. Join some groups and participate in book discussions and takeovers. This is a great way to link up with potential readers. Build a buzz about your book.

I will say it is never too early to start promoting your work. Be mindful that people can and will try to steal your work and pass it off as their own. This can be a dirty cutthroat industry. Make sure that you send off to copyright.gov asap to get your book copyrighted. Don't let anyone else enjoy the fruits of your labor. It is your time to eat!

On IG and Twitter don't be afraid to interact and post about your book there as well. All of this is free promotion. You want your book to be seen! Use this to your advantage. Be great and be humble at the same time.

Good ways to promote your book would be to start your own group on FB for your readers. That is if you have the time. If not interact in other groups to build that buzz. You can do things like short story challenges to maybe get your idea viral. Don't be afraid to share a sample or snippet of your work. Another great idea if you have the title already is to share the title to build up the hype. With a catchy title and one of a kind cover readers will be anticipating the book and sharing it.

Good titles and covers pretty much sell themselves. Make sure to strategically plan this. Always promote your work and your brand. Being that readers are visual another way to draw in potential readers is to do character visuals.

Character visuals are images of the characters with a little back story. Readers love them. It gives them an idea of what to expect with each character. Again the goal is to get the readers anticipating your story.

Lastly, another technique is to create a book trailer. You don't have to break the bank doing this. If you do character visuals just use those and use a free app to make a short trailer or video about the book. Explore all of your options. You want your book to be seen by all. Nothing is better than people sharing your book and eagerly waiting on release day to support you.

All the jewels I am dropping thus far is you as the author promoting your book. This is not even the part where you have paid promoters or paid for ads and sponsored posts. If you have a cover, or synopsis or even a chapter to share by now you most certainly can enlist in the help of promoters to help build your brand. You don't have to wait until the book is out to seek promoters. Just as well as dropping posts and building up your fan base, promoters also have followers and fans, thus exposing your book to even more people.

While promoting your book now would be a great time to start considering reviews. Don't be afraid to ask for reviews! You want reviews for your new book, which will be discussed in the next chapter.

Chapter 6 Reviews

A great book needs reviews. Set up contests for reviews. Simply ask readers in exchange for a free book can they review it. Give away copies of your book to anyone with a blog or website who would like to review it. If you do not have the budget to mail copies, send the e-book version.

Reviews are very helpful to authors. When Amazon ranks your book, the ranking is based on the volume of downloads your book gets and, the number of reviews stacked on the book's review page. Plain and simple you need reviews. Preferably four and five-star reviews!

Word on the street is that Amazon's system is designed to take notice of books that are getting steady traction when reviews get posted. Push for a minimum of at least ten to twenty reviews on release day. The goal is to be seen positively.

It is so critical that when you launch your book you set everything up to get as many reviews as possible to get the momentum going, increase organic traffic, and drive your rankings in the search engines. This means a higher percentage of people writing reviews for your book, not just at launch, but for months down the road. In the back of your book ask your readers to leave a review. When sharing your character visuals, or post about your books please ask for reviews.

The bottom line is, reviews carry big weight in the form of social proof that can drive your book to a bestseller and continue to bring in healthy passive income every month. Get those reviews!

Amazon reviews are great but you could possibly get lucky and have your readers do video reviews that you could share on your social media sites letting the world know how great your book is. Take advantage of it, use those video reviews as free promo as well. Make sure to get your reviews.

Chapter 7 More Promo

By now you should realize that promo and advertisements for your book is just as important as the story itself. Advertise as much as your budget will allow. Pay-per-click advertising campaigns can be an inexpensive way to advertise your book. Link the ads to your book description, with a link to your book on the Amazon store. Services like Google AdWords and Facebook ads charge you only when someone clicks on the ad.

It does not hurt to find a few author friends and cross promote. This is an inexpensive way to promote your book. Make sure to also work it into your budget to pay at least two to three FB promoters. This helps with readers who possibly plan to 1-click your book right then.

On release day, you and your team need to be prepared to promote nonstop. Even after your book is released you need to be promoting at least twice a day. You want to stay just as relevant as your book.

A great way to prepare for your release is to have a contest. Give away copies of your books, tote bags, or buttons and badges to contest winners through your website or email mailing list. You can go live with your book. Create a buzz about your new book. Make people want to download your books.

While you are writing your book you should be promoting nonstop. Let your readers know about your progress. Write and promote. Promote and write. Have fun while doing so.

Chapter 8 KDP

This book focuses mainly on ebooks on Amazon. We can further discuss paperbacks in another book. This book is geared towards reaching Amazon bestseller status in the Urban Fiction categories.

Make sure when you upload your book that you place it in the correct category. This is going to help your book reach bestseller status. Some categories to use are:

African American Urban Fiction

African American Romance

African American Women's Fiction

African American Romance

The Amazon book categories you choose will have a direct effect on whether or not you become an Amazon Best Seller.

Choose the wrong one, and no matter how many books you sell, you won't become an Amazon bestseller. Being a number #1 bestseller on Amazon helps you sell books.

Straight from the horse's mouth, well Amazon's website:

KDP pays royalties every month, approximately 60 days after the end of the month in which they were earned. For example, you'll be paid in October for royalties earned in August, as long as they meet the minimum threshold. You'll receive separate royalty payments for each Amazon marketplace in which you have chosen to distribute your title.

You will most definitely want your book listed in KDP to reap the benefits of good payouts.

Enrolling your eBook in the optional KDP Select program gives you the opportunity to reach more readers and earn more money. You can enroll a single book, your whole catalog or anything in between. Enrolling in KDP Select makes your book eligible for 70% royalty earnings on sales to customers in Brazil, Japan, India, and Mexico.

If you make your eBook exclusive to the Kindle Store, which is a requirement during your book's enrollment in KDP Select, the book will also be included in Kindle Unlimited (KU) and the Kindle Owners' Lending Library (KOLL). You can earn a share of the KDP Select Global Fund based on how many pages KU or KOLL customers read of your book.

Enrolling in KDP Select also grants you access to a new set of promotional tools. You can schedule a Kindle Countdown Deal (limited time promotional discounting for your book) for books available on Amazon.com and Amazon.co.uk or a Free Book Promotion (readers worldwide can get your book free for a limited time).

All authors and publishers, regardless of where they live, are eligible to enroll their eBooks in KDP Select.

When you enroll an eBook in KDP Select, you're committing to making the digital format of that book available exclusively through KDP while it's enrolled in the program. You can continue to distribute your book in physical format or in any format other than digital.

All this information comes directly from Amazon KDP website.

Now that you know how to set your book up, learn how payments are calculated.

The ultimate goal is to reach at least one million pages read a month or better to see a higher payout. This is where it is important to have multiple books or longer books. Get the readers to turn the pages. When writing your book make sure that you are telling a story that your readers won't forget. Write page turners!

By staying consistent and publishing quality books you can make six figures a month easily. Check out your competition to see what they are selling their books for. People don't believe it but .99 books can generate income when marketed correctly. Make sure to write good quality books and be consistent with those releases. I can not emphasize this enough.

Push for at least one million pages read a month and you will see the financial rewards as a self-published author.

For the specific break down of page count and payment its best to refer back to Amazon KDP's website. What I will tell you as an author myself is to publish page turners if you want to earn a living as an author.

Just to recap of what we have talked about so far...

The category and keywords that you create help to push your bestseller status.

The cover and title of your book are very important

The number and quality of reviews for your book

The price of your book matters

The description of your book

Finally, keep on writing. If you write one ebook, that's great... but if you write one each month or each quarter or several in a year, that's even better. The best way to make money with e-books in this genre is to keep the books coming. Not only will it boost the sales of your new books but it will also inspire new readers to go back and buy your older books.

Getting royalty checks that grow each month, will make all of the work more than worth it. You will have mastered how to make money with e-books, and the rewards will be great.

Chapter 10 Resources and References

Because you are hungry for literary success, I've given you the basic tools you need to eat. If you follow my steps and use the resources you are going to have a banger! I guarantee it.

As promised here is a list of valuable resources on the next few pages. None of these services or providers are sponsoring this book. They come highly recommended in the Urban Fiction community. I will list names and you can find everyone on FB. Some names or pages may be changed or updated by the time of this publication but it does not hurt to look around.

Once again congrats on your future urban fiction bestseller. You are on your way to success and wealth.

There are many promoters but these are some well-known promoters in the Urban Fiction community on FB that get results. These promoters are merely suggestions and recommendations. They are not sponsors of this book. Please research and use at your own discretion.

Pages to Like

ZeeHive Promotions

Sizzling Sassy Productions

Secretly-Charm Promotions

Five Star Book Promo

Individuals to follow

Zoya Fryer

Margaret Cooper

Crystal Alexis

Obery Shonda

Vaneka Miles

DeeAnn Orr

Tywanda Brown

For your bestselling novel, you will need a great cover to match the catchy title you have selected. You will also need items such as flyers, bookmarks, shirts, and logos. Here are some great designers. Make sure to check with the designers and ask questions before choosing to work with them. Again, these are just some suggestions. You are the boss and choose who you are going to hire.

FB Groups

She Designs Premades

Black Girls Design Too

Book Covers My Way

Individuals

Jasmine Parker

Chy Seoul

Tina Shivers

Felicia Ann

Navi Robins

BriAnn Danae

Nicole Watts

Jessica Watkins

Iesha Bree

La'Nisha Renee

Mario Patterson

These are just a few of many designers, there are tons! This is just a small list. Please research and make sure to find out which one works with your needs and budget, and most important of all sees your vision. I'm sure that some may be left off the list but in a future book, I will have even more suggestions. Again, make sure you are choosing someone who meets your budget, goals, and expectations in a timely manner.

FB Groups for Urban Fiction Authors

There are so many groups on FB that can be useful to authors in the Urban Fiction community. These are a few groups that are great for an author looking to interact and network with readers. Groups are also a free way to promote. Sign up for author spotlights, takeovers, and discussions. Build up the hype about your book.

There are many groups in FB some are mainly just for promo and link dropping but these groups listed don't disappoint for author support and interaction. As with all things do your research and find out which groups you want to be active and participate in.

Groups to Join

Sisters into Reading and Reviewing SIRR

Talks of the Heart Book Club

Read a Good Book Club

556 Book Chicks

Bookies

Keys No Lock

Black Girls Read Books, Too

My Urban Books Club

Don't Read Me Read A Book

Big Black Chapters

Lady Buzz

Pages to Follow

UBAWA

Bibliophile on A Budget

Again, there are many groups and pages on FB but these are some that have been very valuable and useful for authors looking to network and gain new readers. Most of these groups feature book discussions, takeovers and just great interaction. If you are not already a member join the groups. Make sure to read the rules when joining. Also, make sure to drop an intro post and get with the admins. Use the tools and resources that are available. Positive interaction goes a long way in this industry.

Don't just show up in these groups when you have a new release. Build good relationships and interact as much as you can. You are trying to build your brand and sell your books.

Editors, Proofreaders and Test Readers

Previously I mentioned I would share editors but that is something you will need to research in more depth on your own. That is more of a personal search. In the future after more research, I may be able to give suggestions but for now, I will leave that up to you.

Great editors or the lack of will make or break a story. Do your research. Don't be afraid to ask for samples and ask for a lot of questions. As with all the other suggestions, none of these are sponsored so it would be better as an author to do in depth research for an editor. That would be a book in itself if I started name dropping or listing suggestions as there are different types of editors.

Proofreaders are also good to have but again this is something that you as the author should research to find the person or persons suited to do the job. In addition to editors, there are a plethora of test readers. They can also give you insight before the story is published. Use all of your resources to make your book great. As with anything in the Urban Fiction industry do your research and choose wisely.

As we come to the end of this book you should now be ready to share your bestseller with the world. Follow all the steps in the book and publish your book. By now you should have crafted a well put together book with a catchy title, beautiful cover, a tight description and have readers waiting in anticipation ready to 1-click you right into bestseller status.

Picture this, the readers are loving your book. People are talking about it. It is all the rave. You are consistently dropping quality work and your books are charting. Life is great. Thank this book for giving you tips to use on your journey as a self-published author.

Repeat the cycle all over again. You are now a number one bestseller in the Urban Fiction category. Nothing could be better than this. You set your goals and accomplished them. Pay it forward and tell another aspiring self-published author about this book. Help them on their journey to success. If you enjoyed this book leave a review as well.

Thanks so much for allowing me to take this journey with you. Enjoy the fruits of your labor and the success of being a self-published bestseller.

I feel like I only touched the surface with this book I will definitely be coming with more guides for Urban Fiction authors that go into even more greater details in the near future. Instead of long books on the subjects, I will deliver short books that touch on the subjects at hand. I know time is valuable and of the essence. You have to work on your books so I'll keep the books simple and sweet. If you need to reach me with questions or suggestions please contact me at:

Urbanfictionbestseller@gmail.com

I will gladly answer your questions and post them in the next book. Also, don't forget to leave a review for this book.

Sincerely,

Pen N Paper